10 TIPS FOR A HAPPY AND HEALTHY LIFE

THE CHAIN OF HAPPINESS

10 TIPS FOR A HAPPY AND HEALTHY LIFE

© Copyright 2018 by Marian Hentea-

All Rights Reserved.

This document is geared towards providing exact and reliable information in regards to the topic and issue covered.

From a Declaration of Principles which was accepted and approved equally by a Committee of the American Bar Association and a Committee of Publishers and Associations.

In no way is it legal to reproduce, duplicate, or transmit any part of this document in either electronic means or in printed format. Recording of this publication is strictly prohibited and any storage of this document is not allowed unless with written permission from the publisher. All rights reserved.

The information provided herein is stated to be truthful and consistent, in that any liability, in terms of inattention or otherwise, by any usage or abuse of any policies, processes, or directions contained within is the solitary and utter

10 TIPS FOR A HAPPY AND HEALTHY LIFE

responsibility of the recipient reader. Under no circumstances will any legal responsibility or blame be held against the publisher for any reparation, damages, or monetary loss due to the information herein, either directly or indirectly.

The information herein is offered for informational purposes solely, and is universal as so. The presentation of the information is without contract or any type of guarantee assurance.

The trademarks that are used are without any consent, and the publication of the trademark is without permission or backing by the trademark owner. All trademarks and brands within this book are for clarifying purposes only and are the owned by the owners themselves, not affiliated with this document.

10 TIPS FOR A HAPPY AND HEALTHY LIFE

10 TIPS FOR A HAPPY AND HEALTHY LIFE

TABLE OF CONTENTS

Life Is Yours 5

Be Kind To Everyone Else 8

Take Care Of Yourself 11

Find Role Models 14

Learning To Take Risks 17

Lead By Examples 20

Appreciate What You Have 22

Keep Moving Forward 24

Surround Yourself With Awesome People 27

Plan Your Life 29

10 TIPS FOR A HAPPY AND HEALTHY LIFE

TIP 1

LIFE IS YOURS

Remember when you were a child? Everything you got to do had to come with permission from someone else - your parents, your coach, the hall monitor, the babysitter or any other grown up in charge of your behavior.

If your environment was healthy, you learned to ask for permission and got it when you had proved you could be trusted. If it was unhealthy, you eventually learned to stop asking because the answer was always "no."

10 TIPS FOR A HAPPY AND HEALTHY LIFE

So now you're an adult.

A grown up.

A person with other people in your life you may "answer to" - a husband, a wife, children, a boss, maybe even still your parents. You are responsible to them for the role you have chosen to play in their life.

But don't confuse that with needing their permission.

Your destiny for your life is entirely up to you. They will not give you the authority to be a success - you don't need it and you already possess it anyway.

If you feel like you're waiting for a knock on the door, for someone to tell you

10 TIPS FOR A HAPPY AND HEALTHY LIFE

"Ready, set, go!" you are waiting for a fantasy.

It's not coming.

In fact, it already came a long time ago when you first started your life or perhaps, business. Did you miss it?

The other people in your life would be perfectly happy if you don't change.

But only changing will help you become the man/woman you've always wanted to be. Only changing will get you the lifestyle you know you deserve. Only changing will allow you to build a legacy, a dynasty, a foundation so rich and so abundant that you can shower others with encouragement to do the same.

10 TIPS FOR A HAPPY AND HEALTHY LIFE

You need to change, big change happens by taking daily small steps, and you don't need permission because life is yours. So, get to it!

- What is one daily habit you will start today?

- If you called one extra person each day, what would your books look like in a month?

- What is one food you will stop eating beginning right this minute?

- What is your new bedtime, no matter what?

- If you spoke to a potential client who intimidated you every single day, how long would it take before it came naturally? (less time than you think!)

You were made to run your own life and determine your future.

You were not made to spend the rest of your life in a cubicle helping someone else become wealthy. This is your time, this is your place....and you have all the permission in the world!

Choose your success!

TIP 2

BE KIND TO EVERYONE ELSE

Do you want to be happy? Everyone says yes, but the gateway to happiness makes some of us frown. The gateway to happiness is giving to others. Think about this: "*If you want others to be happy, practice compassion. If you want to be happy, practice compassion.*" - The Dalai Lama

All of us know how a small stone thrown into a pond can stir up ripples all around it. This imagery is a good way of showing how a single person can make a big

10 TIPS FOR A HAPPY AND HEALTHY LIFE

impact on his surroundings and the people around him. It shows how a person and his attitude can affect so much even without his notice or knowledge.

Now think back on how you've been handling yourself and your attitude the past few years. Have you been acting as someone who's been kind and positive? Or have you been acting exactly the opposite way? Remember what you're giving out is affecting you and everyone around you. The great thing about being kind, being loving, and being positive about things is that in return it also always comes back to you.

Whether you've been giving out positive vibes and being kind or being the opposite, here are some things that might help.

Start to live a better life. When people give out negativity and start being unkind, it starts a circle that would often impact one's life. One's relationship with friends, colleagues, and

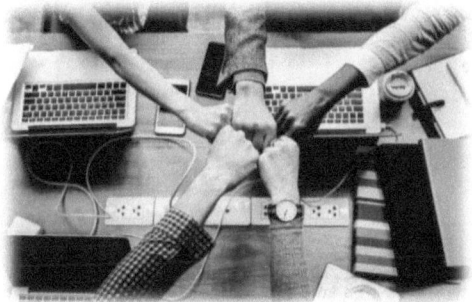

loved ones can be harmed. The best way to get it remedied would be to start becoming a bit more kind when dealing with people. It's a steep road to try to change but starting to recognize how you've been a bit unkind can start you to become better.

10 TIPS FOR A HAPPY AND HEALTHY LIFE

Practice a better way of life. It will be hard to change your way of thinking and dealing with people but often reminding yourself of what you've set out to change will help. Once you start being positive and becoming kind in your dealings with everyone, you'll see it won't only be you who'll change. The changes that you'll start seeing would be having a more positive interaction with people. You'll also see that you'll see less stress in your relationships and less stress within yourself.

Reap the benefits of a better life. Being positive and being loving can start you on a road where you have fewer conflicts and better dealings with everything and everyone around you. It will also feel good to become kind even to those who are being unkind. Who knows seeing you will start them on their journey of change. Lastly, when you start changing yourself, it's not only others who'll love you back, you'll see that you'll also begin to love yourself more.

Remember, all your actions will cause ripples going outwards. It's up to you what effect you'll send out to others and the world. All things are connected, and you can choose to send out love and kindness. Those ripples, in turn, will go back to you.

TIP 3

TAKE CARE OF YOURSELF

To experience happiness and contentment, you must learn to show yourself love. Maintaining a balance of your mind, body, and soul and nurturing each of these is an integral part of providing yourself the love you need.

One thing to understand is that you do have the ability to love yourself. You must believe that you deserve to be loved and that you are a valuable human being capable of receiving love. The sooner you can appreciate and accept this, the sooner you can begin to take positive steps forward.

Gaining an understanding of the connection between your mind, body, and soul is an excellent place to start.

1.) **Take care of your mind.** It's your job to take control of the reigns when it comes to your mind. While negative thinking is common and always has a tendency to pop up, you must fight against it and shift to more positive thinking to provide yourself with the love you need.

- Use your mind to exercise self-control over what goes into your body and how you spend your time.

10 TIPS FOR A HAPPY AND HEALTHY LIFE

- Practice working with positive affirmations to ward against negative thinking patterns.

- Make it a point to surround yourself with good people. Studies indicate that you become like the people you hang around with, so choose your company wisely.

2.) **Take care of your body.** You gain happiness, focus, and energy by concentrating on achieving a healthy body. Taking care of your physical health is equally as important as taking care of your mind.

- Taking part in regular exercise will not only make you feel good about yourself it will improve your body image.

10 TIPS FOR A HAPPY AND HEALTHY LIFE

- Eating a balanced diet and practicing good nutrition will allow you to be full of energy to keep you going during the day, and the better you eat, the better you feel.

3.) **Take care of your soul**. Finding peace and a more in-depth purpose is the driving force of your existence. Getting connected to your soul is integral to finding your happiness.

- Many people practice religion to connect with their spiritual side and feel peaceful. Engaging in an activity that you find meaningful and provides you contentment which will help to strengthen your soul.

- Opening yourself up to life experiences and exploring the world and how it works will allow you to learn new things about yourself. When you expand your horizons, and search your inner self, you become enlightened.

One way to bring your mind, body, and soul into harmony is through yoga and meditation. Going through the different poses and meditative exercises of yoga bring an inner calm and peace and enhance the connection between the mind and body. This is why it has been practiced in Eastern cultures for centuries.

Nurturing your mind, body, and soul will provide you the opportunity to show yourself the love you are seeking and allow you to live a happy more fulfilling life.

TIP 4

FIND ROLE MODELS

The beautiful thing about taking on a new challenge at any point in your life is that there is no end to what you may accomplish. Guidance is critical to help you chart a path and stay on it. Guidance from a trusted source who has been through challenges and persevered is necessary to help you stay the course during challenging times and not wander over to the same dreary path you have traveled before. Habits are hard to break. Mentors will be able to look objectively at your progress and offer a fresh perspective without the bias of your past experiences.

The problem with staying with something predictable is that it may become a deterrent to your happiness if what is predictable is not productive or healthy for you. If you have been in a bad job or a bad relationship for a while, your self-confidence has been depleted. Your sense of normalcy has crept lower every day so that you find that you doubt yourself, you don't see a brighter future, and you figure you might as well just accept your situation because it has become "normal" to you. In a way, you forget who you are and submit to being a bystander in your own life.

How to Find a Mentor for YOU:

1. Find someone with a similar history. Look for someone that has done what you want to accomplish, maybe not on the grandest scale but who has consistently succeeded with innumerable challenges. Look for this person in a company similar to yours that is not a competitor. Look in professional organizations where people with your similar goals meet to share ideas and grow. But also look in non-traditional places. You may find them at

10 TIPS FOR A HAPPY AND HEALTHY LIFE

your church, book group, local pool or gym. If you are seeking guidance on starting a business, governmental agencies such as the Small Business Administration (SBA) or Service Core of Retired Executives (SCORE) may be helpful.

2. Find someone who is interested in helping you. The person holding the greatest success story in the world will not amount to anything for you if he or she does not have time to meet with you and guide you. Spend time talking with potential mentors to find the right fit.

3. Look online for similar stories. Someone in another city may be available to help you via the Internet, but this does

10 TIPS FOR A HAPPY AND HEALTHY LIFE

not substitute for someone with whom you can meet with face to face. People in other cities, though, may not be as fearful that you will be a competitor of theirs.

4. Set up a lunch with a potential mentor. Generally, this will be someone that you have already met and with whom you have a good feeling. If there is someone you have identified as a good potential mentor, and you run into him or her at a social or professional gathering, introduce yourself and share your admiration for his/her success. It is often good to find a mentor within a company in which you may be seeking to work.

5. Send creative instruments of gratitude often. If people do something nice for you,

10 TIPS FOR A HAPPY AND HEALTHY LIFE

you can never thank them enough. Send your mentor a card on Boss's Day that may say, "I know you are not my boss, but you have been a valued teacher and trusted example of success in my life." Send an exciting book that you think he would enjoy. Ask what his or her birthday is and have flowers delivered on that day. Send a homemade treat at Thanksgiving with a note that expresses your gratitude.

TIP 5

LEARNING TO TAKE RISKS

These days, a lot of people are not willing to take a risk. Being brought up in a society were "safe" is better or playing by the rules is seen as smart and good, taking a risk is something that is always seen as a mistake by those on the outside looking in. It's only when the risk taken proves to be the correct or better decision do people simply shake their heads and say "he was lucky" or "good for her, but I'd never do it" and so forth. When exactly did taking risks become a taboo?

10 TIPS FOR A HAPPY AND HEALTHY LIFE

Remember when you were younger and everything was just about exploring, going on an adventure, finding things out and all that exciting stuff? You may not have realized it at the time, but understand now that you were born a risk taker. We all were. It was the only way we could learn about the world, and discover what we can or can't do. For example, we may have never realized we could climb a coconut tree with skill unless you took the risk and just started climbing one day.

So, what happens between our youth and our adulthood? Simple. We are taught and raised that certain things are not worth doing. We're given horror stories of people who took a chance and fell flat on

10 TIPS FOR A HAPPY AND HEALTHY LIFE

their faces. These people, portrayed as idiots, are looked down upon, giving us the sense that if we do the same, we will be looked down upon, and nobody wants that. So, we play it safe, stick to the rules, and live a good, beautiful, normal life.

Then you notice that things start getting boring? Why? Because you've unlearned how to take risks. Your life is entirely safe by societal standards but is no longer satisfactory to your own. So, we look at the children, the rebels, the rogue billionaires who live their lives taking risks, pushing the limit, being different, and still living happy lives. What happened to you? Why are they so different? You secretly admire them, yet

10 TIPS FOR A HAPPY AND HEALTHY LIFE

at the same time, you are afraid to be them.

They are different because they never stopped taking risks. They never unlearned their risk-taking trait as a child. This is what makes them special and unique. They can make a difference through the risks they take because they are different. They see risks as an adventure, a path or road that will take them down a place that some others may not have gone down. They never see risks as a make or break deal.

To break free from safety and monotony, you have to learn how to retake risks. You have to learn how to be curious and spontaneous again. To see life as a road you will only pass through once, so you may as well take in all the sites you can. If your life ends up to be a roller coaster ride, you can always say it was a life well spent. You'll always have a story to tell; you'll always have something you will know better than the next guy.

Learning to take risks is something that can change your life and make it the type of life you've always dreamed of. When was the last time you took a risk? Too long ago? Well, go out there and try something risky. You're sure to come back wanting more.

TIP 6

LEAD BY EXAMPLES

Leading by example is something we often hear about, but how many of us practice it? Consider these scenarios: The "boss" goes home to his family as the team works late on a proposal. The manager sets inflexible work hours while he comes and goes as he pleases.

No matter how trivial the task, the message you will send by simply being there is that you recognize and value the sacrifice others are making. As a leader, never ask people to do what you are not willing to do.

10 TIPS FOR A HAPPY AND HEALTHY LIFE

There is another side of leading by example that many people may not see or appreciate: teaching the next generation and developing your internal talent. On one hand, you don't want your team learning bad habits. On the other hand, you should be aware that your experience likely exceeds theirs, and if you want your team to grow, you need to teach. Teaching, in this case, is often done by example.

If your vision is of a happy, productive, and fun work environment, then you need to be happy, productive, and fun... and let people see it! Some of us with introverted personalities may have a harder time than others with setting this particular

10 TIPS FOR A HAPPY AND HEALTHY LIFE

example. We can be happy, productive, and have fun all in our minds. But we cannot create the desired environment unless we make a visible effort.

So, leading by example is both overt and practiced over and over. Further, the path of leading by example is extremely wide. Beyond the happy, productive, and fun elements of life, there are also opportunities to demonstrate ethical, problem-solving, communications, and empathetic lessons to name just a few. Finally, as a leader, you should realize that whether you intend them to or not, many will follow your example. Why not make it a positive one?

Suggestions

10 TIPS FOR A HAPPY AND HEALTHY LIFE

1. Never underestimate the effect you have on others when you act as a leader. This is especially true the higher you rise in seniority.

2. If you want excellent team performance, demonstrate by example how to be successful.

3. Act the way you want others to act.

4. Be the person you want others to be.

5. Grow (teach) future leaders by demonstrating and sharing your own experiences.

10 TIPS FOR A HAPPY AND HEALTHY LIFE

TIP 7

APPRECIATE WHAT YOU HAVE

If you want to be happier in your life, truly happy, then the easiest way to do this is by altering your thinking. There are ways you can make the most of life. It happens by thinking about what you want from life and what you want to do with that life you have been given. Once you know what you want, you can make a game plan of how you will accomplish this. If you start telling yourself that you were put here for a reason, then you will be closer to making the most out of your life.

10 TIPS FOR A HAPPY AND HEALTHY LIFE

If you want to make the most of life, you do not have to work so hard you cannot even enjoy yourself. The point of life is to be happy with yourself and those around you. You want to appreciate what you have. Everything else will fall into place when you are in this mindset. When you are able to be a happier person, you truly will enjoy your life more. You will no longer sweat the small stuff because you will realize that they do not matter in the bigger picture that is your life. This allows you to focus on what matters.

A great way to make the most of life is to sit and look at what you have in your life. Even if it is something so small and seemingly meaningless, if you love it, then

10 TIPS FOR A HAPPY AND HEALTHY LIFE

it matters. For instance, if you have a family, you can learn to appreciate them better. You will start to become grateful for the time spent together, even if it is just a few hours each day. One of the keys to making the most out of your life is playing up what you have. Make the most out of what you have now.

If you have this mindset, you will be able to appreciate what will come to you in the future. When you make the most of life, people around you will start doing that as well. They will see how happy you are all the time, regardless of the current situation you have. The more people who have this mindset, the better the world will be. Sometimes the best way to make the most of life is by doing something as simple as dancing in the rain or something along those lines.

TIP 8

KEEP MOVING FORWARD

Think about it for a moment....

What comes to mind when you hear this statement? Of course, there is no right or wrong answer to this.

However, the first thing that pops into my mind when I hear this comment is "being resilient." From a young age, I've always prided myself on being resilient and overcoming obstacles. It was drilled into my head that what does not kill me will only make me stronger. Whether it's people or situations, adversity is truly just a part of life. How you respond will make a world of difference.

The next time that you find yourself in a challenging predicament, think about the following tips on how to Keep Moving Forward:

Don't Allow the Situation to Overtake You - Keep busy with what is most important to you whether that is your family, job, friends, or just hobbies. Utilize this time to re-familiarize yourself with what makes you tick and how to be a

10 TIPS FOR A HAPPY AND HEALTHY LIFE

better person. Do an honest assessment of your strengths & weaknesses and always strive to make the necessary improvements. This sounds cliché, but if you look hard enough, there is a silver lining around every dark cloud.

Focus - Think about the solution and not the problem. No matter how much you think about the problem, the reality is that you cannot go back in time to change things. Living with regrets is a natural part of life, but you can't beat up on yourself. You have to know when to let things go. Focus your energy on making sure that your problem never occurs again by learning from the experience.

After doing so, I'm sure that you will find this a better use of your time.

Have Great Surroundings - Some say that "the strong stands alone" but having a great network of friends around is extremely critical in a time of need. This network of friends should be composed of people who wholeheartedly support you and are not just the ones who tell you what you want to hear. Great friends do not come around often so it is up to you to realize who falls into this category so that you can reciprocate the same love and support for them.

Be Positive & Optimistic - The way you view things is everything! According to many books and individuals, some people embrace adversity since it helps to build character. Thinking long-term with your goals and aspirations will help keep things in perspective.

Remember That Success Is the Best Revenge - It's a waste of energy to seek out revenge on anybody/thing that has brought you misery. Just live your life and be happy - I know that it's easier said than done. The fact of the matter is that if someone has intentionally done you wrong, the last thing that they want is for you to be happy. Do not even think about this person and give them the satisfaction. Just do your best not to feed into their goal, realize that the worst thing that you

10 TIPS FOR A HAPPY AND HEALTHY LIFE

can do to this person is to just be happy and successful.

TIP 9

SURROUND YOURSELF WITH AWESOME PEOPLE

"Misery loves company" is a common expression that rings true. People who feel miserable about their lives often gain some comfort when they are surrounded by people who can share in their misery.

When we lack confidence, and have little control over our emotions, we tend to be swayed by the attitude of the people

10 TIPS FOR A HAPPY AND HEALTHY LIFE

around us. When we are around positive people, we will be lifted up by their positive energy. When we are around negative people, we will be pulled down by their negativity.

We should never allow ourselves to be controlled by the emotions of other people. If someone dwells on their problems and is unhappy with their lives, it doesn't mean that we should share their feelings and allow ourselves to become unhappy right along with them. This may be what they would like to happen, but it doesn't help them or ourselves. Remaining upbeat and positive will have a much better impact.

Many people don't even realize that they can control their emotions and remain happy even in difficult situations. We have the choice as to what kind of attitude we will have, and it doesn't have to be the same as the people around us. We can choose whether to be positive or negative.

When confronted by negative people who are angry, upset or miserable, we can choose to remain calm and keep our emotions under control. We should let the person know that we still love them and will support them, but that we will not allow their negative thinking to affect the way we think. They have to realize that they cannot control someone else's emotions and understand that they need to try to control their own emotions.

It is important that we try to increase the positives in our lives and decrease the negatives. How?

• Surrounding ourselves with positive people, places, and things

• Work on building confidence and increasing esteem

• Replacing any bad habits with good habits and reinforcing them through daily practice

• Become a good example for any who has a bad attitude

What kind of attitude do you have? Are you a miserable person or a joyful person? Are you often angry or do you remain calm during difficulties? Do you complain and criticize or do you encourage and uplift? Do you need an attitude adjustment? Attitudes can be catching. What are people catching from you?

TIP 10

PLAN YOUR LIFE

It is an unfortunate fact of human reality that the majority of us do not spend any time in planning the most important things in our lives. For example, do you wake up every day and plan to love your partner more? What is more important to you than your relationship? Surely going

10 TIPS FOR A HAPPY AND HEALTHY LIFE

to the supermarket is not that important but I'd wager that most people make a list and plan what they are going to buy when they are there next.

What made me think of this was a situation which I'm sure many others have found themselves in. We are having visitors and guests for dinner, and some of those guests are somewhat selective in what they will or will not eat. We have spent so much time deciding what to offer everyone that I started to laugh at what we were doing. The amount of energy and brainpower being applied to just FOOD was utterly ridiculous! I mean, let's face it; we weren't discussing a matter of survival, just taste.

10 TIPS FOR A HAPPY AND HEALTHY LIFE

In contrast to this, scientific research has shown the value of a good, close and loving relationship upon one's physical health, not just upon one's emotional well-being. It is a fact that those without a close bond to another human do indeed die younger and suffer more ailments upon the way. Few people expend enough energy on simply intending to love their partner more...and let simple matters of what food they eat or which television program to watch turn into an emotionally charged situation, potentially driving a wedge between them. If an observer were to appear from another planet, they would think that we are insane!

How many more things do we have which are entirely out of perspective? It is a fact that the most decisive actions of our lives are all too often ones which are completely unconsidered.

Perhaps we should all step back for a moment and think about the things which we tend to worry about and ask ourselves; do these things matter? It is likely that most of us expend a lot of wasted energy in worrying about things which matter little in the long term; at the same time, we probably do not focus upon what does matter to us. If you do have an important goal, do you visualize it, see it, hear it and feel it?

www.ingramcontent.com/pod-product-compliance
Lightning Source LLC
Chambersburg PA
CBHW031552210526
45464CB00003B/1273